<u>CHASING F.E.A.R.</u>

7 PRINCIPLES TO MURDER SELF DOUBT

BY AISHA D CREWS

Acknowledgements

My prayer is for God to be glorified in my works and in my life. I am grateful that he chose me as his vessel to tell my story in a unique but God-filled way. This book is dedicated to my Husband, Kevin M. Crews,Sr. Thank you for understanding and trusting this process. To my girls Taylor and Erin Mckenzie thank you both for being there to watch me grow, for boosting my confidence even more by saying you guys were proud of me! My Mother , Regina Jervey and my Father, Robert Jervey, for helping God to bring me about, you both mean the world to me. My Amazing Pastor,Life Coach, Spiritual Mom, and Certified Purpose pusher, Pastor Monica Haskell I love you for never giving up on me and pushing me to see what truly has been on the inside of me! To my Bishop for the countless times you spoke over me and my family, There is no one, like you, I thank God for placing you both and your family in our Lives. To my family and friends for understanding my need to tell my story my way,

Also for understanding that it is my story to tell. For being there during my transition. Thanking God again for this Life, a second chance and for Loving me when I didn't have the strength to Love myself. Aunt Donna and Aunt Nette for speaking joy and reminding me that I do have family when I need them! I pray this book is healing for you like it was for me. It was a Joy to study the word of God and apply it to my life. I wanted to tell my story in a way that it could be used and taught to help people overcome their fears, (False Evidence Appearing Real) Whatever they may be. Nothing is too hard for God. The stories in this book are mine and mine alone, although some weren't all proud moments, I realize now that it was all apart of the plan. God's Perfect Plan. My purpose was birthed out of my pain.

Preface

I read a scripture in the Bible that said "No one will be able to to stand against you all the days of your life. As I was with Moses, so I will be with you; I would never leave you nor forsake you. (Joshua 1:5 NIV)

This Scripture spoke to me as I was on my journey of wholeness. I had to really put myself in a place of solitude for God to be able to work. You see when I was a young girl I was a very lonely child. Although I grew up with both my mother and father one brother and sister they had a life of their own. I had an Older sister as well but we didn't share the same Father. She and I were as close as we could be. My mother was a nurses aid that worked really hard and chose not to go on to college because at the time my father was the one who had went to college and was now supporting the family with his job as an Engineer. Together they were married 14 years. I don't recall them ever being happy, not that they weren't, I just don't have memories of that. I remember them tolerating each other. (lack of an example of Marriage Covenant) I was pretty much ignored as a child in my opinion.

We weren't poor or anything we definitely had the necessities. I just think hindsight they may have been overwhelmed with taking care of all of us and trying to maintain their relationship too. My father also took on the responsibility of raising my Sister that my mom had before they married. I did not enjoy being the babygirl of 4. I had to entertain myself. It was very lonely. We weren't raised to love each other. We were raised in competition of one another. Sometimes I would get into trouble just to be punished, for to me bad attention was better than no attention. I had a principal in elementary school I remember him saying. "If it wasn't for bad luck I would have no luck at all" rude right! I still think about that to this day. That's why you shouldn't allow people to speak negatively over you, but I didn't know that then. I was raised to respect my elders so I never replied. My sister and I were only 3 years apart but very distant in relationship, because of the home situation we shared a room but barely spoke. We went through minor stuff growing up between us but I always admired her strong will and tenacity and never felt like I could measure up. I love my big sister but those feelings weren't reciprocated.

I am sure she dealt with her own stuff but at 6 who understands all of the changes that we're going on around me. I am positive that there were other things going on that because I was the baby no one would volunteer any information. I loved her nonetheless. My Brother was around much but I remember him running away and leaving early on and he became a product of the streets. Thankful that now we are thick as thieves. I believe he had some challenges too with my parents but again there was secrecy. My Father was in my Life all of my Life but he traveled with his job so he was there but in and out, Oh how I loved spending time with him. He had little pet names for me I was his little "meatball" or his "Jive turkey" I would always get excited when he came home from his business trips. I loved getting the gifts he would bring. Our Bond was some what inseparable, I was a Daddy's girl- that is Until the day that changed my life forever.

My parents were getting a divorce, my Father kept the house and all of us kids and My mother moved across town. My father got custody jointly with my mom but we lived with him because she was incarcerated.

My siblings and I soon understood why the divorce happened, suddenly there was a nice lady that daddy started bringing around us. It was his new girlfriend. My soon to be stepmom. She was nice and pretty but she would never take my mother's place, soon found out I didn't fit within her family mold, thus my loneliness began. My father had another child soon after they married, who was another brother for me, and oddly enough I was so happy to have a friend in the house, that's exactly what we were. Things began to change when he was born, his mom began to favor my brother simply well.....because he was hers. She distanced herself from me. We only had dealings when she was punishing me or having my father punish me. She also favored my sister a lot because my sister was their complexion.(thus the Shame of my skin began) when my father wasn't around I was mistreated. I was misplaced and confused not understanding what was wrong with me ? Why didn't I fit?

A short time later I was visiting my mom for the weekend and I had witnessed my mother being taken to prison. I don't really know how I felt when my mother was taken away from me, maybe numb.

I just remember that her and my father had already separated and I can remember being outside and playing when the police surrounded our house and took her and my uncle, who was staying with us at the time, away. So now at the age of 7, I was separated from the one person who understood my quirkiness. I couldn't take it anymore, so I chose to live with my mom even though I knew she was on drugs at the time. It was still better than being mistreated and ignored where I was, My mom was out of prison now I was about 11 or 12 by then. To make matters worse I turned my focus on boys but I wasn't having sex….....

Well not until I was given to the neighborhood dope man as a trade. I remember being asked to go for a walk and her trying to convince me that I had a crush on this man. My mother and I ended up in his house. I thought he was a friend of my mom so I asked could I use the bathroom, only to come back to a locked door and no parent. (Innocence stolen, Trust is now broken) for any person in my Life. If I can't trust my own mother who could I trust? I didn't have a relationship with my sisters , it was on and off never consistent. I do have a close relationship with both of my brothers.

However, I never told anyone what my mother had done so I just buried it. I had no self Love it was tough having to deal alone. I didn't feel loved. I didn't understand all that was happening to me.............I do know my entire life had just shifted.......

Isaiah 12:2 Surely God is my Salvation. I will Trust and not be Afraid. The Lord, The Lord himself is my Strength and my Defense. He has become my Salvation.

The Prayer of Salvation:

Heavenly Father, I have waited so long to invite you into my Life, but just like the thief on the cross it's never too late! I know that I have sinful ways and without you I can't be saved. I need you in my Life, I will Listen and obey when I hear your voice. By faith I gratefully receive your gift of salvation. I am ready to trust you wholeheartedly as my Lord and Savior. Thank you Lord for coming to earth, dying on the cross so that I don't have to endure the sins of this world. I thank you Lord for rising on the third day. Thank you for bearing my sins and giving me the gift of eternal life. I believe your words are true. And I give you permission to tell me what to do! Come into my heart, forever more In the Mighty All-knowing All Powerful name of the Lord Jesus, Amen.

CHAPTER ONE
THE RUNAWAY

How does one discover the life that God has for them? How do you know if you're living the life that you're supposed to live? At what point do you stop making excuses and blaming others? Why was I even born? Why did this have to happen to me? How do you fix what's been broken? How do you erase the pain of your past? At what point do you stop settling for what you know is not God's will? How do you know that it's not normal to be in an abusive relationship when that's all you saw? How do you shake the feelings of loneliness when you're within a relationship ? How do you stop being the person that they want and become the person that God has designed you to be? When is the right time to forgive? How do you know that you have completely forgiven? What do you do when you hate everything about yourself? Who do you tell that you don't feel that you are good enough? Who do you tell that you feel insignificant? Why do you walk around smiling when inside you are slowly dying? Who is gonna Love me?

Have you ever wished you had a different life? A different family? A different face or Name? These are just some of the questions that I had asked myself while trying to find out exactly who I was in God. The enemy would have you to believe that life will be easier if you leave everything and follow him. So he attacks us in our minds he wants us to **Forego Everything And Run!** (F.E.A.R.)

What is a runaway? A runaway is a person who has left something or someone, to leave quickly in order to avoid or escape something, to bolt, to gain a substantial lead, to win with a large margin. That's precisely what we need to do RUN! Far away from all the negative things.

I was alone during this journey. I was afraid during this journey. I once had thoughts of suicide. I was afraid of what people would say and think of me all the time. I couldn't allow myself to open up to anyone long enough to build trust. Life just didn't matter it seemed no matter what I did it just didn't seem good enough, to me. I have always had this expectation for myself but I could never quite touch the why? Or where the feelings came from. Who they came from , how they came about, and when I was going to arrive at this place of peace.

I was tormented sometimes by myself and sometimes from the devil. It started at an early age when my innocence was stolen and I lost trust for the person who was supposed to help me become a woman. I also lost Trust for Men because of the rape. This book was not supposed to be about me totally it was supposed to be empowering to help other women murder self doubt, self-hatred, self-loathing disappointment, disgust and any other vile word you can think of to describe yourself much like I did. I fell for the tricks I had to say NO to the devil I am running from you, I just want to live.

YOU CAN'T HAVE MY LIFE. I realized that in order for you to understand I have to be transparent. I began to think about everything that I have been through in my life. I began to remember while these events were very traumatic and very disheartening probably some things that the average person wouldn't live through , I smiled because I survived. I didn't lose my life, I survived. By the Grace of God I Survived. With all of these questions that I had looming in my head I still couldn't figure it out and for the life of me, I still didn't know how to find a genuine ounce of appreciation for what God has done for me. I hadn't given my life over to him yet.

I didn't even know where to start, Instead I found self pity and depression. Why me? I would ask God why did I have to endure such pain and heartache? I got saved when I was an infant but that was out of tradition. I needed to invite God in now that i'm older, I want to get to know him for myself. I did finally get saved again when I was around 18 or 19, but even though I didn't get saved before then by a preacher my Step grandmother and Grandfather saved me because my pop-pop was a Pastor. I am so grateful for them both then and now. Today I'm a different kind of survivor. I now know that in order for me to be healed and whole my perspective had to change tremendously. I will be eternally grateful for everything that God had allowed me to go through. I now understand in order for me to help young girls and women with being battered or raped I had to go through it so that I could be a true witness to God's deliverance. God has been there with me every step of the way and has shown me how to be a blessing to myself now and to others. I begin to examine myself and my life and I wanted to do it in such a way that the person reading this would hear my heart and understand that even though I am imperfect I learned how to trust the one that is perfect.

The seven principles that I will give you in this book will not only guide you to becoming a better person, it will help you get to know me as a person. The ultimate goal is to develop a new way of thinking.

I love what God has done in my life and because of it he's teaching me how to teach others. Some of these things I have never told anyone in my family. Some of the things I endured only me and my abuser knew. My family knew I had experienced some stuff but not all of what I am going to unload, I am encouraged to help heal people who have suffered or are suffering from similar life events. I knew that I was going to have to deal with my past in order to bring my vision into fruition. I hid a lot of stuff most of the time. I was not living, I was existing only, if you will. One thing for sure and two things for certain I have a Newfound Love for God now more than ever in my life and I'm all the better because of it. For it's important to know that sometimes you have to lose something to gain something better. I lost my sense of self but I gained a relationship with Christ.

HOW TO BREAK AND IDENTIFY A
GENERATIONAL CURSE

First things first let's define what a generational curse is, simply put you can not break something if you have no idea what it is. A generational curse is anything that has occurred in your family multiple times and has not expanded the value of it but rather brought damage or harm to it, more or less presented itself " as the thing" that is just inevitable to happen. Pastor John Edmondson of New Jersey once taught a sermon that Generational curses come from Men. He says "Women do not have the progenitor gene to pass anything down especially sin. Women are the incubator to what is given to them and because she can't give Seed she is therefore not the Progenitor. Women can only give birth to what is given to them. Women can receive a thing, incubate it, multiply it and give it back." So somewhere down the family tree a man in your Lineage(grandfather,great grandfather or father) has done something and has therefore brought a curse or damnation

on anything that is connected to them. I would define it as
having come from what some believe, as the situation when a
relative within the family tree did something and it brought
misfortune or bad luck on the family.

Generational curses are not Biblical but God can and will
help you shut them down Indefinitely. Generational curses
are to be denounced starting with us by calling it out ! We
already know that anything that is wrong or bad does not
come from God. So this must mean we were taught this
behavior and way of life. We may be doing things
unknowingly, and it may have been a coincidence to
something that may have been a pattern in your family
dynamic. One huge misconception when it comes to a
generational curse is that we have even been taught sayings
like" you will do what your parents do" or " you get it from
your mama" we have seen in society time and time again
that many mothers got pregnant as a teen, therefore their
daughters are also going to get pregnant as a teen. It's been
said that alcoholism is passed down. So you might have
heard a person say "my father was an alcoholic that's why I
drink to fix the pain of my problems.

When actually it's the opposite alcoholism or any type of substance abuse for that matter makes your situation worse. So while I totally understand the generalization of the saying "you are a product of your environment" I do not agree. And the Good News is , you actually don't have to be. Life is full of choices and decisions.

I was not brought up in the best home environment but my parents did the best they could. I chose to fight for my freedom. Why? because I am worth It! Trust me I didn't get it right for a while but now I know better and I want to pass on the knowledge I have gotten along the way. It took me a minute but I decided early on I would be the Runaway in the family to get far away from the curses that were written into my future. The first sign that I needed to keep pressing was that my mother was pregnant at 14 and yes I too became an 18yr old teen mom. My mother dropped out of school in the 8th grade and so I surpassed her I dropped out in the tenth grade- no generational curse here right? LIES! We both later went back and finished but the ideology was there. Who was I fooling this was not even when I realized I needed a change I was comfortable making my bad decisions. So when I heard the Pastor speak on this I was blown away!

The information that I mentioned above from Pastor John Edmondson ,I now had an understanding of this means.

My mother obtained her curse from her father(my grandfather) who gave it to her mother(my grandmother) in the form of seed (my mom) and it was incubated and birthed and multiplied (me and my siblings). Unless one of us denounced this curse it would have continued. I chose to be the one to Denounce it! In Jesus's name. I will tell you later on how I overcame adversity and decided to go back to school and finish and obtain a few degrees. There is so much more I want to share with you on this topic. I just want to make sure that I properly lay the foundation for you, so that you can not only get the mental understanding but also the visual understanding. I want to draw a picture for you to let you know that life is not all about roses and lemonade. It's different for everyone. Some people have to overcome one obstacle after another. While others are seemingly going through life without one hiccup. When you allow God to guide you, your life will be easier to understand. Don't get it twisted just because you are saved doesn't mean you are free from the devil's attacks. It's actually multiplied. Because now he sees you as a threat.

He does not want you to get what God has for you. He can see what God has for you, and frankly if he can keep you from it he will. The bible says that no weapon formed against us will prosper. It doesn't say the weapon won't form. It says that when it does it won't prosper against us. Life is choice driven. The Lord gives us free will and common sense. The bible is an instruction manual (The Word of God) for life. Let's see what God says about any curses within the Bible-The bible mentions generational curses several places within -but a few scriptures comes to mind Exodus 20:5 , Exodus 34:7, Numbers 14:18, and lastly Deuteronomy 5:9. Basically it tells us of how God is a jealous God, and he is punishing the children for the sin of their fathers to the third and fourth generation, to those who hate me he says. It sounds really unfair for God to punish children for the sins of their fathers. But there is more to it than that. The effects of sin are naturally passed down from one generation to the next. When a father has a sinful lifestyle, his children are likely to practice the same sinful lifestyle. Which was Implied in the warning of Exodus 5:20, basically saying the fact that the children will choose to repeat the sins of their fathers is upsetting to God, the key word here is choosing.

So, in all actuality it is not unjust for God to punish sin to the third or fourth generation those generations are committing the same sins their ancestors did by choice!

Sometimes as women/men we may be brought up in a household where there's a lot of emotional tension there is instability on your parents part. Maybe Mom is the culprit mainly because just maybe that's what she was taught and she did not know any better. When we go through emotional fear, untreated it later develops a spirit of fear the fear of the unknown.

Romans 12:1-2 says I appeal to you therefore brothers by the mercies of God to present your bodies as a living sacrifice, holy and acceptable to God which is your spiritual worship, your reasonable service to God. Do not be conformed to this world, but be transformed by the renewing of your mind, that by testing you may discern what is the will of God, what is good and acceptable and perfect.

If we look intently at this scripture it says that we must treat our bodies as a living sacrifice, so if you are inviting unhealthy behavior and mistreating your body that is not showing gratitude to God. He isn't pleased, he wants you to denounce these curses.

The very ones that have been passed down for four generations. So if we think about these terms pertaining to it being a curse or curse-like, then yes absolutely that type of behavior is a curse. As children we are taught whatever morals and values that are parents have instilled inside of them. My mother for instance didn't know how to be a mother because her mother was taken from her at an early age. My Grandfather murdered her due to drug use.(death of relationships, curse of substance abuse) So that shaped her entire future. She did the best she could. Those unfortunate things are said to become our habits , our addictions, and our daily way of life. The way we learned how to cope with certain things. So in order to properly explain what a generational curse means to you, you would have to do some introspection and take a look and examine yourself and your family and their life. Do a genealogy tree. Find out what things happened that were repetitive in your family that you can remember, do this to get to the root of the challenge. I strongly believe the challenges are meant to be overcome, I have been taught to never use the word problem because it is seems so final. It seems like there's no way to fix it, but if you have a challenge than most certainly it can be fixed.

It can be repaired. So, that's the word that you'll see me use a lot throughout this teaching. You can not pray down or cast out a generational curse like you would a demon. Curses need to be Denounced, (Ephesians 4:27) the definition of the word denounce is to publicly declare that something is wrong or evil and must be unwelcome. I also saw in the scripture that God follows it with which is your reasonable service, meaning this is the very least that we should be doing, living holy. When your spirit is unsettled or your heart is filled with fear you are not in worship to God you are in obedience to the devil. Two things about fear are you are either running from it or running to it! Fearful of what? That is the question that we want to answer why am I afraid? what do I have to be afraid of? Those are some very good questions that you should ask yourself in order to gain a better understanding. To be unsettled in your spirit may cause torment and may trigger a series or a pattern of behavior. Examples like maybe making a bad decision , maybe not thinking long enough about a decision that you have to make, doing things that will cause you to self-destruct. This becomes an inner struggle something that's going on within the inside of you it becomes almost an internal warfare.

It makes you extremely frustrated. I will tell you this anger, frustration, self-destruction, and indecisiveness, are all the things that satan will try to implant in you and you must know they are definitely not from God. So now we have to ask the inevitable question where is it from? I don't even want to acknowledge the devil in my writings but it is the truth he will subliminally plant these things on the inside of you because he sees that you are not strong in God yet. Two very important words that come to mind are confusion and depression those are both results of family curses and they go back as far as we can remember. Simply because again it comes to morals and values that were instilled within our parents. If they were not instilled properly then that's what they're going to do, pass them down to you. That's what they know and that is what makes it a generational curse. Knowing what I know now about it is the reason why a person may be indecisive and have challenges lining their life up with the word of God. The first thing you need to know is this does not have to be your life's assignment. The cure for a generational curse has always been repentance. God responds to obedience.

I want to encourage you that things will get better.
Sometimes you gotta give up what you think you have in
order to get what you really want. Then other times God will
remove people and things from our lives that we are not
strong enough to remove ourselves. In the coming chapters I
will help you from start to finish how to identify all of the
signs and symptoms of a potential challenge. I will introduce
to you seven principles on how to murder self-doubt,
self-loathing, communicational issues, social withdrawal, and
how to properly have a genuine relationship with members of
the same sex and of the opposite sex. Relationships are very
important in life they help us grow if we cultivate them just
right then we can have them for a lifetime. The priority is
becoming the best version of ourselves that we can possibly
be, with God's help. In order for us to become the best
versions of ourselves it is imperative that we get to the root
of what's going on. We all have certain behaviors certain
habits that are not very good. Things that that make us
perform less than what our God-given value says that we
should be and do. I mean there's no perfect person but surely
each one of us can individualize ourselves and just say you
know what because I do this it's making me behave like this.

This cycle must stop. The bible say all have sinned, and fallen short of the glory of God Romans 3:23. So together we will run swiftly away from all those challenges that hold us back. We will Run Away from anything that is not God's will for our life,that being said I am ready to give you principle number one.

PRINCIPLE#1 GET TO KNOW YOU! THE ONE WHO GOD DESIGNED AND PREDESTINED YOU TO BE. This is Detrimental to your healing process. To do this find out what makes you happy, Be daring and try new things out. The theory here is for you to weed out anything that is not pertinent to your destiny it has to go! Make a list of Goals for yourself. **(Jeremiah 29:11-13) For I know the plans I have for you, plans to prosper you and not to harm you , plans to give you hope and a good future. Then you will call upon me and come and pray to me, and I will listen to you. You will seek me and find me when you seek me with all of your heart.** We must Learn to **Forgive Everyone And Repent!** (release your fears)

CHAPTER TWO
<u>THE EVICTION</u>

Eviction is defined as recovering property from a person by legal process. To drive or force out; to force someone to leave a place; to eject,remove, dispossess, dislodge. Can you think of something or someone you need to evict from your life? The first thing that comes to mind is The devil! Evict him, with all of his trickery, lies, and deceit, satan YOU GOT TO GO! How often do we rebuke the devil but invite him right back? We so often fall for his corny temptations, sneaky ideas and vile invasion of our minds. A random thought of failure, a sneaky scheme to get over. A flash of that movie you know you shouldn't watch, suddenly your co-worker never looked so good because things aren't lining up at home with your spouse. A lesbian or Homosexual thought implanted in the minds of our children making them think they are supposed to be gay or bi-sexual. All of these things are examples of how the devil lay in wait to attack us at the very core of our being. Always in the area of our secret challenge. The Bible says in John 10:10 for the thief comes ONLY but to steal and kill and destroy!

But it doesn't stop there : God says but I have come that you might have purpose in life and have it more abundantly. A rich satisfying life. We must Evict the devil send him back to the pit of hell where he came from! The enemy will have you to believe that you are good for nothing, ugly, friendless , that no one loves you. He will try to make you have a deficit in life. A life filled with fear floating over you like a cloud is your norm. LIES!!!! This is the fear that he tries to put in us Let me show you how we can defeat the enemy and EVICT All of the stigmas that we are challenged with. Let's look at Emotional Fear.

BREAKING DOWN THE STEPS TO EVICT EMOTIONAL FEAR

Are you challenged with neglect, rejection or misguided feelings of affection? The first thing you have to remember is that your life should not be completely contingent upon just your emotions alone. We are human beings and it is important to function as such so yes you will have feelings about certain things.

Our mind, our body, our intellect, our will, and our emotions should all be guided through the Holy Spirit. The Holy Spirit was a gift to us from God Almighty. As Christians we need to learn how to tap into and utilize the Holy Spirit.

Depending on where you are in your walk with God, you may understand and know about the Holy Spirit. You may have knowledge about how he was left behind through Christ that we might need a helper. I encourage you to employ the Holy Spirit in your life. I was one that I literally had to be broken down to the last fiber of my being before it dawned on me that I had not been utilizing the Holy Spirit to my advantage. I thought that I was but when the rubber met the road I was not seeing Manifestation. I like to think of my relationship with God as a mature Christian, but I haven't always been that way. You see, I was very emotional in a sense that I lived off of the way things felt. If things didn't seem right, if they didn't look right then my mouth would confess the reality of the situation and we know that isn't nor was it going to be right. I would allow the devil to plant thoughts in my head, to punk me and before long, I would be confessing the very thing that I had just heard. The devil does that he will have you thinking it was your thought.

He is only doing his job, so you can't be mad at that right? Wrong. The Bible says the thief comes but to steal, to kill and to destroy, and we are collateral damage when we allow him to succeed. I would often times base my relationships solely on how they felt. If the relationship felt good then we were good. So often we place conditions on our relationships and as long as the conditions are being met then everything is fine. When It got difficult I would leave. I wasn't staying and seeing things through, I would just move on to another relationship male or female, friendships or a boyfriend, it didn't matter to me. Then I would sit and wonder why my life was so chaotic. I had to learn to teach myself through studying the word of God that in spite of what happens in life I have to make sure that I live my life as unto God. I simply could not drag baggage from one relationship to the next. So let's define emotional fear it is defined as a feeling of induced by perceived danger or threat that occurs in certain situations or events. Fear is a chemical imbalance it causes change in our metabolic and organ functions, and ultimately results in a change of behavior. A sudden feeling to flee, hide or to simply freeze in place. We've already covered the fact that we know that fear is not from God.

That fear was created by the devil to attack our minds to make us think that we cannot achieve something. Emotional fear is a stronghold. If you are not careful it will give birth to something else. Strongholds are meant to be broken, omitted and cast down. **Fear- is False Evidence Appearing Real.** The Emotional side of it to me comes from the personal impartation that we allow in our lives. This unstable connection we tend to hold on to every hurt, every offense that people do to us. The problem is we hold onto it when we should be releasing them. Why would a person hold onto something that is harming them? I did it as a reminder not to let it happen again. Only that seemed to be the only type of people I attracted. Hurting people attract hurting people. When we say we love a person we care for them and do for them. We say this relationship really makes me feel good but at the end of the day what happens when it doesn't make you feel good? Do you disassociate? do you detach from that person that we say we love? The answer is depending on how serious the relationship is you may have to, but if this relationship is a marriage then no you can't unless the other person is physically harming you. I have been through so many unsuccessful relationships.

As much as I would love to sit around and tell you that it was their fault and not mine I would be telling you a falsehood. Honestly people, we just carry our baggage from one relationship to another without doing housekeeping. Our house is our body, the temple that we promised God we would take care of. Ultimately the end result is we have now developed an emotional fear of relationships with a stigma that the next one won't work either. I can remember having a relationship with a young man and we were friends. We weren't really that serious we were actually just dating, but in my mind we were exclusive. I was so desperate for someone to Love me, I bought his love or so I thought, so that was the first two issues, because one we never had the conversation about what our relationship was and two I bought him stuff and assumed he was all in. When there was actually no commitment and loyalty. When I caught him cheating and spending his time with someone else I was hurt. The Challenge here is this is a guy I was dating for a little over a year, I thought it was relationship and I immediately attached myself to him and made my claim. I never dated I just had boyfriends. There is a difference. When you date you have friends that you hang out with no sex involved.

You get to choose who you spend time with, no pressure
until you find the one that you have the most in common with
and from there you decide mutually what you want to do.
When you have a boyfriend you guys are exclusive hence the
title. Neither one of you is seeing anyone else. For me to be
that emotionally attached to someone is really a little
abnormal. Ok a lot abnormal. As a single person you can
enjoy spending time with somebody hanging out but if you
guys never had the conversation of exclusivity then you
really can't get upset when things don't go the way that you
anticipated they would go. It's important to have
communication in any of our relationships whether it's with a
good girlfriend, boyfriend, your parents and your siblings ,
your spouse, or co workers. Communication is key it helps
you develop a positive relationship with the person and a
level of trust with them then, there will be no room for
emotional fear or unexpressed expectations. I will say my
emotional fear started back when I was younger I lost my
sense of trust for people- I would say women mainly because
the person that I trusted the most let me down. My
relationship with all of the women in my life was strained
severely.

I got to a place where I shut out anyone who tried to get close. My lack of trust for women turned into a lack of trust for Men. Thus my judgement of others was formed. To me they were all untrustworthy. I had an unhealthy example of what dating looked like. My mother was involved in a few dysfunctional abusive relationships so I thought that was what Love was. I thought when a man hits you then he must really love you. So that's where I ended up. In an abusive relationship with my oldest daughter's father. He saw how I didn't have much guidance at 17 and took advantage of that fact. It didn't start out that way but it ended that way. He would beat me, rape me, and make me do things for him and to him that were not acceptable. I wanted to be in this relationship so bad I was willing to accept anything, even abuse. There was no self-Love or self-worth. I would clean his apartment so he wouldn't be mad all the time. I would cook his dinner if he liked it he would eat if not he would throw it out. He was 21. He was a little older than me and had a good job as a truck driver with his own apartment, I assumed he would take care of me. He was to be my Knight in shining armor. To take me away from everything that had happened to me in my life.

He was my God- I worshiped him. God is a jealous God I was committing a grave sin. He had his own gun and a huge Love for weekend drinking. He was not my Prince Charming. I didn't see that originally. What I saw was a way out of my mother's house. A way out from all of the drugs she was doing, drug addicts that would constantly be in the house. Not even our house. The house we stayed in was the house of a "friend of the family" who lived in an Atlanta . I was the surrogate mother to my little brother, because I wanted to make sure he was taken care of. My little brother who I later found out was not my Little brother at all but actually my cousin that my mom raised but that's another story. I met this young man and he was my way out. I decided to move out and Live with him, leaving my brother/cousin behind. I would bring my brother over from time to time. I wanted a different life so I ran into the arms of the first man that would have me. He would drink and want to fight with me then I would get beat. I remember I stayed in our bedroom for days on end not allowed to come downstairs unless his mom was coming over so we could seem normal? Why would I stay you ask? What else was there? My mom? My Dad? I chose to play house.

I have a dent in my head to this day because I was hit repeatedly with a 9mm just because he could. I was in constant fear for my life. Everyday never knowing was today gonna be the day that he went too far? I Should have been dead. But God Kept me. I should have been complaining less and rather confessing the opposite of that by speaking that all things were created for the good of them who love Jesus. Instead I continued in self pity. I sowed seeds of discord in my own life and I created unnecessary drama. I was bitter about what happened to me. I began to sow seeds of doubt, seeds of hate, and seeds of unhappiness. I got away, finally and went back only to get away again for good. In all actuality even though these things happen to me God and the Holy Spirit both were there but I didn't tap in and therefore, because I did not I could not reap the benefits of healing my mind. To have fear within your emotions simply means that there is a disconnect. The disconnect could be the fact that you don't know who you are in God therefore your confidence is broken and you spend majority of your time trying to be someone that you are not. Trying to find someone to fill that void.

From everything I have learned from my past, that at some point in your life you have to stop making excuses and just decide to be happy. God is everything you need him to be. I begin to form alliances with my abuser because he was my daughter's father. He was never a bad dad, he was just a bad boyfriend. My stepmom and I began to heal as well. I was finally old enough to tell her how I felt about what she did to me. I was able to get it off of me. She admitted that she didn't know how to be a mom to me. That was enough for me. I had already forgiven her. My relationship with my mother was healed also I had to forgive her in order for my life to be renewed. I forgave her because my well-being was at stake. I understood that it was the drugs controlling her and not her in her true self that allowed those things to happen to me. She has been clean now for over 25 years and I couldn't be more proud of who God has made her.

HOW TO MURDER THE DEAD WEIGHT WITHIN

I needed to Lose weight. Not physical weight but the weight of my past. We need to Lose Weight in order for us to be healthy in our mind, body and soul.

Do you need to go on a diet? Mentally, spiritually or an actual physical diet. We are obese and slowly dying because of the food we choose to eat. The food we let others feed us. I am not speaking of physical food but the food of the spirit. Some of us will eat anywhere. Let anybody feed us, Instead of choosing to eat where a little word will get you full. We choose the smorgasbord. We must be mindful who we allow into our lives. We must be mindful of who we allow to speak(feed) into our lives. I heard a statement once by Minister Shea Fleming she said "In life people speak things over us but it is our responsibility to either receive it or reject it" that statement alone speaks volumes about the baggage that we invite into our lives. Once you receive something negative or positive you now have ownership.

You can do two things keep it and walk in it or release it and Murder it. The decision to be happy is exactly what it sounds like, a decision. We must make a calculated decision that we no longer want to live without the guidance of the Holy Spirit and just Live!!!! Truth be told once you get to a certain age and maturity it is your responsibility to be accountable for you and everything that you do. Every word that you speak comes with responsibility.

I want to encourage you in this chapter not to do what I did not to wait so long before you tap into everything within your reach. I urged you if you're having these feelings and you have displaced emotions and you're not sure what to do with them my best advice would be to seek counseling. I know, I know it's a stigma counseling is for crazy people. I know specifically in the African-American community we're taught that counseling is not for us. Black people go to church. Following this old tradition you are doing yourself a very huge disservice. Although, I can't be in every single home and tell all of the parents how to raise their children I can help them with my own story. Here's my story we'll part of it anyway. Learn from it and grow from it. God created therapists for a reason he must've known that somewhere sometime we would need some counseling, someone to talk to. Someone that has a specialty in the area of whatever challenge you face. I know, I know yes we do have the Holy Spirit that is when you pray and seek relationship with God and yes we do need him everyday, but get yourself a Christian therapist too. The Christian therapist is tangible help and can pour into you in a professional and spiritual way.

You may have so much going on and so many thoughts in your head that you can't think. He/She may be able to help filter through some of the those things. There are a lot of tools that a Christian therapist will help you with or introduce to you to help you on your journey to wholeness.

Just begin to thank God for not taking you out in whatever situation you are dealing with. Begin to express sincere gratitude toward the creator himself. I had a situation happen once in my life where I was being taken advantage of and because I so desperately wanted to be in a relationship I allowed it to happen. We have to make sure that we're just not allowing anything just for the sake of being a part of a partnership. I totally had a fear of being by myself. There was always someone in my life. I needed to draw nearer to God. It's very important that we learn to understand that having an attachment to emotional fear is dangerous. It has multiple personalities, and will only make matters worse. Always remember people can only do to you what you allow them to do.

The second principle for emotional fear I would say that it is imperative- to get rid of it! Get it away from you, don't be a part of it! Remove its very existence from your life.

Basically anything that will put you in a place of emotional fear or can make you do and say things that you may feel are detrimental to your health is a dangerous road to travel. I urge you to give your life to God and ask him to help you remove it. Every lesson that I've ever learned in my life I give the credit to God. For the people that he has placed in my life and that he places in your life with a message. I have mentioned earlier that even though I have known God my entire life, I have never been taught the principles and the teachings and the illustrations, and having actually put feet to my faith until much later in my life. I am a member of Prevailing Church International in New Castle, De and I have never joined a ministry where the Bishop and the Pastor alongside their entire family literally are living examples of what Faith and God-given Prosperity looks like. Because of their love and reverence is so great for God they were able to model, demonstrate, and display what genuine love looks like. What the calling of God looks like in a person's life, because of that I'm eternally grateful. I'm glad that I received it even if it was later on in life because it's helping me now. It's giving me the strength now to be the woman that I am.

I now know how to let go of all of my displaced anger and fear to release my emotional fear and replace it with unconditional Love and understanding that God is the creator of all things. God is the provider of all things. It is evident that you continually tap into his grace. So that every hurt, every ailment, every sickness and every disease will line up and be acceptable unto the word of God. God died on the cross for us to not have to live and worry about all of the things of the world. And it is because of him that my Pastors are able to teach the way that they teach with such passion. It's only because of God that they even are are here with us today so I'm grateful for them teaching me what I needed to know to help myself and anyone connected to me. My Bishop Matthew C.Haskell,Jr always says "The difference between you and the person sitting next to you or standing next to you is the application of faith." How you walk through your journey using faith. We don't get in fear we get in Faith. we already know that faith was given to us at Calvary. So in order for us to activate it we actually have to be a doer of the word and not just to sayer. You don't have to tell people that you are a Christian, they should see it in you. By the way you talk and treat people and behave.

You have to physically show love. You have to physically do the work so that you can reap the benefits that God has already supplied. We were all created to have Dominion over all things! There should be nothing in our lives that is too large that we feel we can't move it with the words that we speak. Our words shape our future. Therefore I decree and I declare that I will be free from emotional fear for the rest of my life and I will apply my faith to every situation and challenge In Jesus name Amen.

PRINCIPLE #2 EVICT EMOTIONAL FEAR FROM TAKING UP RESIDENCY IN YOUR HEART AND REPLACE IT WITH THE LOVE OF GOD. (Ephesians 5:15-18)
This step is imperative without it you will continue to revisit the issue. Do it for your health!

CHAPTER THREE
THE PURSUIT

Pursuit is defined in Webster as the action of following or pursuing something or someone.
an effort to secure or attain; a quest.

Romans 12:2 says *Do not be conformed to this world, but be ye transformed by the renewing of your mind, that by testing you may discern what is the will of God, what is acceptable and perfect.*

This is the pursuit that God would have us to chase, not F.E.A.R. When there is a pursuit of God there is a spirit of gratefulness you begin to feel **Freed Encouraged And Renewed.** I began to have a calmness come over me as I started the pursuit.   At this point I did not want to be outside of God's will. I was Hungry for him to change me and to do a work within me. I studied his word and changed my speech. I had to change the way I behaved. I just wanted him, nothing else. No more immaturity and childish behavior I had to grow up and become a mature Christian.

Part of my plan was to just make a lifestyle change. At first I had to guard my eyegates and ear gates. I could not just watch anything on tv or online. I could not just listen to any kind of music. I wasn't ready to invade my time of worship. I couldn't have people speaking negatively around me. I wanted only pure thoughts in my head and heart. I was so sensitive at this time that even people around me had to respect where I was and if not they had to go. I am still this way and have vowed to stay this way forever. This was the time to pursue Holiness in God's Fear. To chase God in a steadfast pursuit. What a privilege and a joy it is to pursue and serve God!

Joshua 24:19 says *then Joshua said to the people "you are not able to serve Jehovah,(if you serve other Gods) for he is a Holy God. a jealous God demanding what is rightfully and uniquely his. He is a God who requires exclusive devotion. He will not pardon your transgressions and your sins."*

"Other Gods" in this passage refer to anything that you love more than God(money, sin, a person or material things). The thing that is uniquely and rightfully his is us! He wants us to live our best life yet free of sin.

Free of greed but full of obedience, purpose, faith, prayer and manifestation of his promises. Most importantly addition to the kingdom. Why would we want hoard God all to ourselves! Spread the Love and Joy of Christ and allow someone else to feel how you feel. This is why I am sharing and encouraging with everyone because at the end of the day your testimony is not for you it's for everyone else! God didn't allow you to live through all that you have been through for you to keep it to yourself.

Everyday is another day to pursue God, another day to get it right. But don't be stuck! You actually need to get it right. Make your faith more than just trying to stop wallowing in a world of sin, but rather a desperation to get to know God on a deeper level. This makes me think of a time where I was straddling the fence, I went to church and bible study but I was still deep in sin (I was in college) I had an experience with a demon. Because the calling of God was on my life so strong I can remember waking up after I had an been out clubbing and partying all night long with people who I was in school with, so-called friends. Well my roommate had just left to grab breakfast and coffee and shortly after I saw this demon sitting on my bed laughing at me.

It was as real as real can be. He said to me " you are the biggest hypocrite! You are a joke! You need to come all the way over to my side because the road you're on is dangerous, you pray and we hear you! You shout and we see you! You even tithe, but yet you still partake in irresponsible behaviors." I was mortified! Now you know when the evil no longer perceives you as a threat it's dangerous ground you're walking. I knew in this moment that nothing good was in my future if I kept this up. Step out of your comfort zone and allow God to completely transform you from the inside out. Allow him to bend your will, renew your mind, awake all of your dead senses, clean up your conscience, break your heart so he can mend it. Allow him to give you a clean slate. Allow God to alleviate your judgement. Allow him to soar within your spirit and create in you the man or woman of God that he predestined you to be from the time you were in your mother's womb. God is able to do just what his word says it will do. He will Fulfill every promise to you but you first have to know what God promised in his word. If you don't know what his word says then how can you be effective in prayer? You have got to read and study his word so that you will be armed in times of adversity.

PURSUING HAPPINESS

Happiness is the state of being happy, to find pleasure, to be content, to be satisfied, cheerful and to be full of joy! Let God do that in you! Another one of my challenges was I hated the way that I looked. So I was always either gaining or losing weight. I was a career dieter. I don't believe there was a diet out that I didn't try. I would diet and get to my cute place and then stress eat because I was truly unhappy with the me on the inside. See, for me it really didn't matter as much to me what I looked like on the outside but that's what people saw. So I had to care about that too. I had to put a front like I was happy. I always had look the part. Put on nice clothes and makeup and hair had to be right. Even when I got skinny I still found a million other things wrong with me. So all of the Covering up served no purpose because I was still empty on the inside. I would begin to allow the devil to minister to me and feed me negative thoughts about myself- from the dent in my head because I was abused by my oldest daughter's father, or the way my stomach was filled with rolls etc.

This is unhealthy behavior. This is another reason why it's important that you get to the root of any emotional challenges that you might have, because it will help you stay focused on the prize. Much like a drug addict is addicted to drugs or an alcoholic needs his little taste, food was definitely my addiction! I had an unhealthy relationship with food. I was an emotional eater. I ate when I was happy, sad, celebrating, mourning lol ok I'm greedy but don't judge me. It really is an unhealthy habit. When I got to the root of my why, I found out that it was linked to relationships or the lack thereof. It stemmed all the way back to when I was a kid and my parents divorced, I would get treats from them both to make me happy. I wasn't a fluffy kid I actually was very skinny but we bonded over food. Then as I got older my need for sweets and fatty foods increased with every failed relationship. I would eat to get through the pain of the rape. I would eat to get myself in/out of depression. Which when I was younger I didn't know it was depression. It was tough **Finding Empathy After Rape**. I became bitter and cold. Back then I wasn't taken to a therapist for it, this is why now I am on my journey at such a late age in life.

I **Fought Every Attempt Religiously**. It took years to finally own my challenges and begin to pursue change to them.

Psalm 37:4-6 says

4 *Take delight in the Lord and he will give you the desires of your heart.*

5 *Commit your way to the Lord and he Will do this.*

6 *He will righteous reward shine like the dawn, and your Vindication like the noonday sun.*

In other words he will make you BranNu (Becoming Righteous Authentic Natural Neoteric and Unique) Neoteric is another word for new. I needed to become new. I needed a new attitude, a new perspective on life. I needed a heart transplant. God began to do that in me. I started a company called BranNubyaishaJ, Aisha J was the girl all of this stuff happened to, so I had to attack it at the head. My company is everything I wasn't growing up. A foundation for young girls and women to learn about self-esteem, hygiene, speaking, growing and keeping healthy relationships, and mentoring.

I felt a shift one day at church I was singing on the praise and worship team and our leader was going after God, I remember asking God for that Fire! I asked him to show me how to decrease and increase in HIM. He replied " study me , get to know me and you will see I have been there all the time." I yearned for the chance to just really go into a sincere heartfelt worship. So I began praying Gods word back to him and whenever I got the opportunity I was praising him on a deeper level. It was Me and him No one else! I have always listened to worship music but the songs seemed more intense and personal now. I asked God to sharpen my vocal skills so that the next time I got the mic I was gonna really show him my love and affection without fear. God began to work because I wanted it as much as I wanted to breathe. I longed to have purpose and live a life with meaning, I wanted to know him. I was finally on my way to happiness. There was a calm and a peace in my spirit. Those around me begin to benefit. I learned that Offense was an option. Whenever things don't go your way or someone does you wrong you have the power! You can choose to be offended or not. My Bishop says that a lot and It's the honest to goodness pure TRUTH!

Do you know how hard it was to lose that trait? Man! I had an answer before they even knew I would be offended. Have you ever done that? Have an answer to a question before the person was done asking? It's another setup from the devil. He will cause friction and build that lopsided house of strife. It is very evident that when the devil bothers you so much that there is a calling on your life. I know that now but looking back I thought I had a target on my back. Even our founding fathers knew how important it is to pursue happiness, we will find that within the Declaration of Independence of this great country this was told to us to have Life , Liberty and the pursuit of happiness. All it takes is a simple decision to be happy. This seems easy enough right? I thought so. I would find positive affirmations and post them throughout my home, my car Just to serve as reminders who I was and that I am walking in happiness. I began to dwell there. That was very peaceful and infectious at the same time. A person could not be around me and be angry or unhappy. I would give them a reason to be grateful. Now that I see clearer there is no way I would have made it without the Love of God on my side. That's why I love him like I do.

That's why I pursue God like I do. I Chase after him like he stole my money and I want it back!

Philippians 4:11-13(NLT)
Not that I am speaking of being in need, for I have learned that whatever situation I am to be content. I know how to be low and I know how to be low and I know how to be abound. In any and every circumstance I have learned the secret of facing plenty and hunger, abundance and need, I can do all things through HIM who strengthens me.

When my kids were young I taught them this scripture to say if they ever felt defeated or confused whether they could complete a task or not. They still recite it today. Matthew 5:8 says Blessed are the pure in heart for they will see God. This scripture resonates with me, my heart is pure now and it was partly because I sought after him and learned to allow the word of God to fill and penetrate my heart. I learned to meditate on the word , and trust in everything the word says. Simply put The Word Works! The word empowers you to excel in life. When people say the Bible is a manual for life, it literally is.

PRINCIPLE #3 PURSUE GOD WITH YOUR WHOLE HEART! Never be content with Mediocrity. But be Content with the Lord for he will keep you, and Elevate you as he sees fit. A Strong foundation and Covenant with God can help you on your journey to pursue Happiness. Find the strength deep down in your spirit to know you are beautiful/handsome, You are Intelligent and pull your self esteem and self worth back up again! Try to Get **Familiar** with **Exalting And** having **Reverence** for God.

(Embrace your Fear of God, to fear the Lord is to worship him)

CHAPTER FOUR

<u>THE WALK</u>

On Dictionary.com they define to Walk as moving a regular
and fairly slow-moderate pace by lifting and setting down
each foot in turn, never having both feet off the ground at
once; an act of traveling or an excursion on foot. proceed by
steps; move by advancing the feet alternately so that there is
always one foot on the ground, to go on strike;to conduct
oneself in a particular manner; pursue a particular course of
life.

Colossians 3:1-10 tells you exactly what to do to begin your
walk:

since you have been raised to new life set your sights on the
realities of heaven. Where Christ sits in The place of honor
at God's right hand. Think only of the things of heaven not
about the things here on earth. For as a believer you died to
this life and your new life, you're real life is hidden in Christ
through God. So put to death all of the sinful earthly things
that are lurking within you. Have nothing to do with sexual
immorality impurity lust and evil desires.

46

7

It goes on to say: *don't be greedy for a greedy person is an idolater a worshiper of the things of this world. Put on your new nature as you learn how to know your creator and become more like him.*

I was beginning to get excited about my walk. My Walking away from the old and Walking into the new. Walking away from **False Evidence Appearing Real** and Walking into my **Freedom Entitled Approved Rights** as a believer! My Life was at stake. I needed to do put one foot in front of the other and make a change! I walked right into my destiny! God welcomed me with open arms **With All Loving Kindness.** (He showed me how to walk)

Every worry, Every unfortunate thing that I have ever been through it was all worth it! During this time I was so appreciative of the fact that God chose me. He chose me to show forth his Glory with a miracle. That miracle was me! I was on my way to walking with God. I came to a place where I never want to be outside of his will. I don't want to tell a lie, I don't want to curse, or argue or fight!

Once I was in a convenient store and I went in early in the morning.

I got my coffee I got some fruit and I had a bottle of water as I was gathering all of my items I put the bottle of water under my arm so that I could carry everything.

As I went to the register I paid for my coffee I pay for my fruit and I even paid for a pack of gum . I get to my car to put everything down in my front seat as I journey to work and I realized I still had his bottle of water under my arm. Now the average person would have said oh well I forgot I'm not gonna go back in I'm just gonna go ahead and go hey free bottle of water! But not me this time of my life was so sensitive that the very thought that I could steal something or that I did something wrong was completely out of the question, so I held my head high I put a smile on my face and I utilized my integrity and I walked back into the store and made it right. I Walked back in the store to the register waiting for my turn the young lady said "you're back again?" and I replied "yes ma'am I most certainly am I didn't even realize that when I walk to my car to put all of my items down I felt something under my arm and I realized I had his bottle, so if you will allow me to I would like to go ahead and pay for my item and I apologize for walking out with it."

The young lady replied "WOW, God bless you because I can promise you the average person would've kept going and said hey I got a free bottle of water." I replied to her "I love God too much, I need him too much to allow a bottle of water to come between he and I" she just smiled and so did I. Listen I don't want to mistakenly take something because in all actuality I would be stealing something from myself. That is how much you should value your relationship with God that not even the most minute thing she come between you and him.

I think Casey J said it best *"it's more than a feeling, it's more than emotion, and it's more than just a moment in time."* God wants to give, speak and love us more. She says *"I'll take this moment to seek you, I'll spend a lifetime to love you and if it takes eternity just to know you then I know you're worth it." God is the King of Love and he's waiting to Deliver.*

I totally agree with the song, in a sense that building a relationship with God is more than going to church and dancing, singing, and shouting.

If you come home from a church service and don't remember what the word of God was that was preached and ministered or you didn't take notes for later reference, it might be safe to say you are still stuck in the feeling of church rather than the principles and lessons that can be learned and taught. That is if you belong to a teaching church. I believe it does matter what church you go to and it does matter who your Pastor is. You don't want to just go to church out of ritual or tradition you need a relationship worthy of testimony. How will you grow the kingdom of God if you don't take the time to get to know the God who keeps you? To take it a step further your Pastor can be the baddest Preacher this side of Heaven but if you aren't disciplined enough to study God's word on your own or even know that as believers we have weapons that we can use for everything to guard us from attacks from the enemy. I had to really get to a place where there was no choice I had to go after God myself. I had to speak life over myself. I had to encourage myself. Once I knew the tools in which to bring anything into Manifestation It propelled me forward.

At this stage you should be well on your way to total and complete wholeness in God. This walk is so special, it's more special than anything that you or me has ever experienced in our lives. The Bible says that all have sinned and fallen short of the glory of God that's Romans 3:23.

So the sin that was brought upon me, and the sin that I committed myself; I thank God that he is not holding it against me. That my life can be new. That my mouth can speak into existence anything that lines up with the will of God and his promises for me. All I have to do is open my mouth and pray to the father in Jesus's name and any thing that I require or ask it shall be given unto me. Did you know that God has given us dominion over all things? All things! not just some. But know this, you also have the power with your mouth to kill, to destroy, to weaken, to harm yourself or the people around you. Take your responsibility seriously, understand that the Bible says the power of life and death is on your tongue- Proverbs 18:21. The mouth is a tool that is used for eating, and for speaking so we must utilize it wisely. We have the power to do anything and bring anything into manifestation with our mouth alone.

Imagine the day when you actually become a doer of the word coupled with right speaking! The Power of God will be glorified and the devil will be horrified. So if it's weight you need to Lose speak it from your mouth and do the work and you will receive. If it's challenges you need to overcome speak to them and they will be removed from your life. Sometimes as believers we have seasons of doubt. As humans this is normal but should not become a part of our lives as a believer. It should be put in check. In the seasons of doubt we somehow talk ourselves right out of our blessings. When we doubt we negate our prayers and God can not move where there is doubt. We talk ourselves out of manifestation. We talk ourselves back into the same rut. We talk ourselves into negative situations into situations that will not prove God's glory But actually speak against it. Sometimes we are praying to God and we're asking for specific things but deep in our conscience we have just a small inkling of doubt, even though it's small it's still negates our prayer. Our thought life is so important. We have to pray in confidence knowing that at the very moment that we are praying we have received it. I say simply find what you want in the Word of God and pray God's word back to him.

Knowing with Confidence that no matter what the reality looks like we are asking the father in Jesus's name and we already have the very thing that we're praying and asking God to give to us. God responds in prayer when you know his word. That is the very definition of faith. Believing that you have a thing before you can see that thing, this is the only way to achieve God-Filled manifestation. I believe that I have made it through this journey. I believe that I am delivered from pain in my life. I believe that all of my relationships are restored through the glory of God. I believe that my children are the very manifestation of my hard work. I Believe that my Husband is the Man that God has called him to be just because I prayed. I am reaping the benefits of his covenant with God. Do you see a pattern here? I am using present tense. Why? Because Faith is right Now! Faith is present tense. Faith is happening Now, not later. We have the power for Faith to work in every area of our lives. Faith can go before you when prayer becomes a way of life. Being a Christian isn't just a religion it's a way of life. A lifestyle. Think about it this way it's similar to getting rid of habit that you know aren't good and because you made a decision to change it and you did the work it changes.

It's the same thing it's just replacing the Worldly behavior with that of Christ-like behavior. We will still make mistakes but at least now there is a Covering on our life, and tons of benefits just because he loves us that much!

Walk this thing out! Take it one day, one step at a time. Start small like making it a habit to read a scripture every day. Meditate on that Scripture allow it to live in you. If you have to begin to keep a journal of your scriptures and write down what it means to you and how it can be a present help to you now. Make a list of some goal that you have, pray about a way to bring them to fruition. Be like Nike and Just Do it! Remember you and anyone connected to you are the beneficiary of your hard work. Go back to the basics look at the definition of walk. To walk means to walk in a slow-moderate pace but moving forward. You will never get anywhere in life looking back. Truth be told you might run into something if you aren't looking forward. Yes it's true that you must grab challenges from your past and evaluate them so they can be overcome but don't stay there. Get past the strongholds that have you bound. Be Free In your Mind, body and soul.

Can God Locate you where you are? Is your relationship with God able to know or discern when you have disconnected from the father? What words are you speaking on this walk that will bring Life to a dead situation? Or are you not watching what you speak because you wanna blend in? What would your friends and family say about your walk? Would they say she is one of us? He is part of the crew? Or would they say that you are different and you stand out because of your love for God. Everybody can't go with you, so don't allow your relationships to become so familiar with people that you compromise your faith, just to be a part of the group. You are not like everyone else. God said you are a little "G" meaning you were created in his image and his likeness therefore you are different and you can't be common. You are not average. My Pastor says "Never shrink back who you are to make average others comfortable." If people are around you they ought to want to be great too. It shouldn't intimidate them. It should motivate them! People are watching. So make sure you show others what a Christian looks like. That means No you can't go out drinking. No you can't go to the Casino gambling. No you can't do anything that would jeopardize your witness!

Unless you are going to these places to grow the kingdom and witness and you are not partaking in the foolery then that's different. We are all former something or another's and somebody got us saved so the best way to be effective is to show God's love in demonstration. Model it for others so they can know that God is the reason why you are so happy, whole and complete.

PRINCIPLE #4 TRUST YOUR WALK WITH GOD, FOR IF GOD BE FOR YOU, IT'S MORE THAN THE WHOLE WORLD AGAINST YOU! Romans 8:30-31 says and having chose them he had called them to come to him. And having called them he gave them right standing with himself. And haven't giving them right standing he gave them also his glory. What can we say about these such wonderful things? If God is for us who in the world can ever be against us. no one can separate us from the love of God. Colossians 3:16-17 let the message of Christ in all his richness fill your lives. teach and counsel each other with all the wisdom that he gives. Sing psalms and hymns and spiritual songs to God with a thankful heart.

Whatever you do or say do it as a representative of the Lord Jesus Giving thanks to him through God the father. Again I remind you that the Bible is a living word breathing manual of life with this you can live a new life! The life that God has ordained for you to Live Free from sin, fear, frustration, indecisiveness and anguish!

CHAPTER FIVE
THE RACE

Webster defines the word race as a competition between runners, to compete with another or others to see who is fastest at covering a set course or achieving an objective. To move or progress swiftly or at full speed.

Philippians 3:12-16 says not that I have already obtained it this goal of being like Christ, or have already been made perfect but I press on so that I may take hold of that perfection, for which Christ took hold of me and made me his own. Brothers and sisters I do not consider that I have made it on my own just yet but there's one thing I do: Forgetting what lies behind and reaching forward to what lies ahead. I press on toward my goal to win the heavenly prize of the upward call the higher calling of God in Christ Jesus. All of us who are mature pursuing spiritual perfection should have this attitude. And if in any respect you have a different attitude, then pray that God will make it clear to you. Only let us stay true to what we have already attained. Knowing this I am running full speed ahead into the arms of God. I need his protection.

I need his angels to be dispatched specifically to me. I need him to allow the Holy Spirit to guide me and teach me the right way to live.

In June 2016 my husband and I were on vacation in the Caribbean island of Jamaica Montego Bay to be exact. I knew that prior to us boarding the plane that I was overcoming a cough I had a tickle in my throat so I did everything that I could possibly do to try to read my body of this cough. Prior to boarding so that we would have an exceptional time. We were celebrating his birthday. While on the island somehow my cough has progressed it was very persistent it would not let up so much so that I could not enjoy a slushy or any other cold beverage not even water to be exact I was drinking peppermint tea which is a popular drink in Jamaica it has healing power. My waitress would make it for me every time we sat down to a meal. Now mind you we are in Jamaica so it's 80+ degrees outside and I'm drinking hot tea. I'm about to paint a picture for you you going to think you were on his island with us. I try to enjoy myself only to end up in bed for one full day while we were on vacation but my husband understood that I needed to be strong and I need to get better so he allowed me that day.

When I finally decided to get up and go enjoy myself maybe
you know soaking in the water because their salt water so it
has healing powers as well we noticed A woman who had
taken in too much alcohol and she had the bright idea to get
into the Jacuzzi so as we are watching her meeting a nurse
and my husband being a firefighter and EMT, needless to say
we sprung into action because she slowly slipped under the
water everyone around us was trunk no one was paying her
any attention except for us, I said all that to say that even
though the drinks were unlimited my husband overcame
alcoholism and I don't drink so we were able to still enjoy
ourselves on vacation without partaking. I thank God that he
kept both of us because we were able to help save this young
woman. As the medical workers scurried to her side and to
our side they begin to bring out a machine known as an AED
which basically is an electro shock machine if someone you
know is having cardiac arrest however this young lady was
not, and she was wet! While she did pass out we could see
her chest rising and falling which meant she had passed out
but she still was alive.

The medical staff of the resort still proceeded to attempt to connect this woman to the machine after several onlookers and us told her she's not dead! After witnessing this horrible encounter with the medical staff and how they treat the customers, I had decided that I was not letting them put their hands on me. So I said God you gotta help me right now from this cough because God forbid I have an asthma attack they don't have the equipment to help me. So I held on literally in that same moment this young lady said that her son had a nebulizer and that her and her family were from Delaware too and that if I needed it, I could use it! Look at God! I held on after that treatment and all of five days later when we return home I go to the ER, I remembered I had asked God to keep me while we were on the island, my cough and asthma tack have turned into bronchial asthmatic pneumonia. I go to the ER they give me all of the medicine that I need to get better and at the end of my visit they tell me please follow up with your primary care physician. Now I will stop the story right here just for a moment just to insert some information that I later found out about myself. It is highly imperative as human beings to not neglect ourselves our bodies our families.

What I'm about to tell you next is not hard for me but it's disappointing for me. So I went to the doctor's office two days later because it was a Saturday when we returned and doctor's office open on Monday. When I go into the office, I was given a nebulizer. I was given a prescription to get some more inhalers. I had to get some antibiotics and I had to get some steroids. Right as I'm about to finalize the visit my doctor turns to me and asks if I would like to get the mammogram that's been in my chart for four years. (I work for this hospital and I know without a shadow of doubt that we have most certainly changed computer systems 2-3 times, so it was hard for me to fathom how this order for a mammogram remained in my chart for 4 years) so keep that in mind as I continue.

I told my doctor sure I'm off for a little bit overcoming from asthma to get my breathing back together so yeah I will go ahead and I'll get this mammogram.

So a little background for me in 2003 I had an abnormal mammogram and while, it did come back benign the mass ended up being like a little cyst, but because they were in such a weird place and the fact that I was young, not really the age for a mammogram.

The doctor insisted that he remove them and will keep a
close watch on me. I had at the time been given instructions
to continue to get mammograms every year to keep myself
healthy. The doctor that I had at the time gave me an
instruction to continue to get mammograms every year to
keep myself healthy. So the fact that this mammogram have
been sitting in my chart for four years is proof to you how
easy it is to forget to neglect yourself when you're taking care
of your family and others basically everybody else. I went to
get the mammogram on June 23, 2016. I wasn't worried or
concerned because they always are negative, I mean even the
reason I had to start getting these so early was because of a
cyst that presented itself as a mass. Which we later found out
was benign.

I got a call later that day that they would like me to come
back in for a diagnostic mammogram because they saw
something that was not worth overlooking. So I scheduled to
go back the following day June 24, 2016 and I have my
diagnostic unilateral left breast Mammogram. While I'm
there I'm thinking that we are finished but the technologist
tells me that yes they do see something suspicious and if I'm
not in a hurry they would like to do a diagnostic ultrasound.

They wanted to see if they can get a better look at whatever this is. So again I agreed I was so accustomed to having these test done and the results be negative that even in this moment I still wasn't concerned I wasn't worried. So after the ultrasound was completed the radiologist was now there and he asked me to go ahead and get dressed, he wanted to review then speak to me with clothes on. So I take myself and my belongings down the hallway to the office and he comes in to explain to me what they think they might see and also asked could I go down the hall to the breast surgeon office. I needed to make an appointment to have a consultation with one of the breast surgeons because of what they found on the ultrasound and both mammograms they needed to now do a biopsy. So I go into the surgeon's office to find it empty but one girl up front and someone at the fax machine. So I begin to explain to the young lady why I was there and she checked the schedule only to see that none of their doctors had availability within a few weeks to a month. Suddenly the man at the fax machine says " I'll take her, put her on my schedule for tomorrow" and he walked away. I asked the girl who was this man?

She giggled and said that's Dr. Witmer, his wife owns this office but the funny thing is he isn't a practicing physician here . He works out of St. Francis. Sometimes he fills in for her and i'm assuming that is why he just offered to help you. (pause) So wait this mystery Doctor shows up at the fax machine the very moment I walk into schedule and there are no appointments available! (God is already orchestrating his move) I start smiling and I hear the Holy Spirit tell me " it's okay I told you we got you" I know exactly who it is that I trust , and it's the God in me. I trust him with every fiber in my being. I did not know what type of Journey that he was about to take me on but I was eager to find out. So I followed instructions I scheduled an appointment. I met with the surgeon all in the same week and I scheduled to have this breast biopsy on June 27, 2016. I was in total faith that I was fine. I was totally prayed up. When it was time for me to have the biopsy , I had to just remove the clothes on the top half of my body. Then replace them with a gown. I was greeted by the ultrasound tech and she explain to me what her role was going to be. He then comes in and tells me what he is going to do, where he going to do it and that he will numb the area.

As they begin the test I begin to feel what he was doing on the inside of me. I said "hey doc I may need some more numbing medicine because I feel you pulling." He replied its ok im almost done. The sounds of the drill were magnified, I quickly recognized that the devil was trying to implant fear on the inside of me. So I quickly snapped back and said you're right! I will be still and I begin to pray again as the tears were now rolling down my face. I realized in this moment I would have to walk this journey alone just me and God, Because even though my husband is a Firefighter and EMT, He saves lives for a living I knew I had my Faith ready to be employed for him because this was something he couldn't save me from. I had to run this race and see it through. Now the testing is done and we are waiting for confirmation of what was found on the mammogram and ultrasound. I had to wait a few days for the report to come back, and that was on July 1,2016 I believe when I went initially went back to the office. However; on June 30, I looked in the computer I saw all these words written under my pathology report. I just skimmed down looking for the word *Overall Impression* to see what terminology was used.

The results read: **Left Breast Invasive Ductal Carcinoma grade 3, estrogen and progesterone receptors negative, Her-2 (FISH test to be determined)** for me to see this exact terminology was surreal because I have been an oncology nurse and I knew the terminology from when I had worked in Cancer care, in Atlanta. So when I saw that it said invasive ductal carcinoma it threw me for a loop it was almost like I couldn't believe that I was reading this report that was attached to my name. I begin to search for more info by going further down the page because I wanted to find out if this is true. What are they saying it is? There was no mention of the staging. So I'm like what's going on? Then I played dumb and I called the office and I asked if the doctor could call me because I was waiting to get the results of the test. When he didn't call back right away I asked the young lady to please page him in the OR for me. He called me back, He told me to keep my office visit that he would speak with me and my husband and family once I got to the office the next day. All of this was happening so fast but I remembered what the Holy Spirit said to me so I was content.

So I just did not claim nor accept what I had read because in my mind I was in the wrong chart. I had to prepare myself for tomorrow and believe that what the doctor was going to say was in-line with what I believe.

When I got to the office the next day he came in and he greeted my family. I knew he was nervous because he had the look of death on his face. He goes to the computer and pulls up the finding on the biopsy, slightly he turned around his little chair and he says to me "so the report came back positive for breast cancer on your left side and your estrogen was negative and your progesterone was negative." (basically exactly what I had read previous) He proceeds to tell me normally and medicine negative is good but that we are still waiting for the third part of the pathology to come in, this form of negative was bad.

So he gave me two scenarios one was that knowing the size of the tumor. If the third part comes back positive then while it's still bad news, we would have more options. On the other hand if the third part comes back negative while its still bad news it lessens the survival rate because the treatment options are slim to none, so there is a chance that I will lose both of my breast.

The doctors did not want to take a chance in having it spread or metastasize. He repeats himself and says "not in this case we are still waiting on one more part of your biopsy to come back it's called the HER-2, it's another part of your hormone receptor levels which tells us whether or not your particular type of breast cancer is hereditary or not. If the HER-2 comes back positive then you are considered to be in the normal class of breast cancer patients in which case it's said to be hereditary, and there are tons of options of treatment. If it comes back negative your treatment options have become slim. Oh and I almost forgot it's a stage 3 grade 3. As he got up and walked away.

PRINCIPLE #5 LOSE EVERY EXCUSE AND LEARN TO RELY CONFIDENTLY AND CONTENTLY ON THE LORD WITH ALL YOUR HEART AND DO NOT RELY ON YOUR OWN UNDERSTANDING OF THE REALITY IN FRONT OF YOU, BY DOING THIS IN ALL YOUR WAYS ACKNOWLEDGE AND RECOGNIZE HIM AND THE LORD WILL DIRECT YOUR PATH (my interpretation of Proverbs 3:5-6.)

CHAPTER SIX
<u>THE C.H.A.S.E.</u>

To chase is defined to pursue in order to catch or catch up with; or try to make contact with (someone) in order to get something owed or required. I decided to Chase God by Choosing Happiness And Success Everyday. As I continue my story , walk with me.......

Ok so let me get this straight not only are you telling me that you see an invasive ductal carcinoma but you're telling me that it could potentially be triple negative which there is no cure for, which is also very rare cancer which it 1 out of every 9 people that get this maybe black women but it mostly attacks hispanic. This is said to be non hereditary and you are saying death is inevitable? And you just gone slide in there it's already in a stage of terminal? I said to him I see what's on the paper and I hear you saying the words out of your mouth but I need to let you understand that from this moment forward I will not say it. I will not claim it. It does not belong to me. I trust the report of the Lord.

Needless to say a few hours later I was called and told that yes my HER-2 had come back negative. It was in this moment I felt connected to God more than ever. I wanted answers, but I knew the doctor could never give me. I had to use my knowledge of Oncology medicine. I had to step back and examine everything around me. I had to trust God solely, because science was not about to help me Jesus was! Suddenly, the noise was loud around me. The doctor's mouth continued to speak to me on the phone. I Heard nothing. I was at work and all I could think about was how this man has just changed my entire life. My life was not going to stop like this. I had not fulfilled purpose or changed my destiny. This was not acceptable! This was Disrespectful! I begin to process the information I had just been given. I then realized I had no one to call and speak about it. Here I was being told that I was the distressed owner of a Triple Negative Breast Cancer, non-hereditary and terminal. I then asked for genetic testing to be done because I wanted to know why, where did this come from. So I met with the genetics team I paid for my test and I had my blood work drawn. So now all I had to do was wait…. wait to hear if these results were also positive or negative.

In the meantime my surgery was scheduled for a double mastectomy and my next group of providers would then be my Oncologist and chemo nurses. My doctor went on vacation and my surgery was not for another three weeks this was go time. This was the time to not only say a prayer but to activate my faith by speaking healing, by speaking cancellation and by confessing that my life was already bought and paid for by the life of Jesus Christ.

This was a lot of information to take in. While I would love to sit here and tell you that I did not have a moment of weakness I would do you a huge disservice to lie to you. I am perfectly imperfect. I am human. So the day that I found out happened to be a Thursday, it happened to be a day that we have Bible study at my church. My husband and I agreed that we would not mention it to the children or to family because we were confessing and believing that by faith I was already healed. My children and I share a tight bond and I felt like they could handle hearing rather than me just not tell them what was about to happen. So on the ride to church I had a chat with them and told them the doctors are concerned about me and they are running some tests.

I explained to them that mommy had a mammogram and they saw something suspicious and that we were going to all be in faith that it's not Breast Cancer like they think. My oldest is 20 and she just gave me hug and said "mommy you are a child of God i'm not worried!" My heart melted because of both of my girls she is the cry baby, so I was surprised she was being strong for me. My youngest showed absolutely no emotion at all and this worried me because she is my loveable huggable one. I was genuinely concerned for them both. How do I explain to them that it's gonna be okay? How do I convince them this too shall pass? So with all confidence in God I explained what I knew from the word to be true, and I was firm in it. Nevertheless I went against what my husband and I had agreed to do and told them both. I walked into the church I smiled at the greeters I spoke to a few people that were on standing around and down the hall comes our youth pastor, Pastor Lauren. She said to me "Hey Sister Aisha, how are you? You good?" and she gave me a hug (this was the moment everything that had transpired over the last week had hit me) I fell in her arms and I cried in her arms she asked me what was wrong.

Even in that moment I didn't think about it then but now I know where my heart was I responded to her by saying "they said I have breast cancer, they said I'm going to die, they said there is no cure, and they said to prepare my family." Immediately she sprung into action she asked me to go into the overflow room she got permission from Bishop she pulled Pastor Monica from what she was doing and together they prayed with me, they encouraged me, and they reminded me who I was. They laid hands on me, and they covered me with anointing oil. They armed and prepared me for the fight that needed to happen. They told me to remember that I was already healed they asked me to pull every scripture in the Bible on healing and recite them daily, they asked me to write a confession for myself for healing and recite it daily. They asked me to surround myself with people who are like-minded that believed in God the father Almighty that his blood was shed for my sins and My healing and that by his stripes I was healed! So I did just that! Now while all of this was going on with me, in the sanctuary I was later told that my Oldest daughter entered the sanctuary and the minute she hit the door she fell.

She began crying and praising God for my healing! YESSSS GOD you better use my kids! My youngest still holding back but I know God will minister to her as well, she is very strong. Knowing that my family was behind me I began my race to the father!

I knew in my heart that everything I had read in God's word was confirmation to my spirit and it needed to be activated NOW! So I was now I'm prepared armored up ready for my fight of faith! My surgery was one day away I went into that building with such confidence and cockiness because I knew that God was going to perform a miraculous work in me! I am the miracle that God has performed.

One night I tossed and turned ad simply couldn't shut my mind off by this time it was prior to surgery and about 6 weeks before Chemo was to begin The Holy Spirit had another message from God:

Today should forever be in your heart. God has shown you that above all else HE LOVES YOU! He loves you so much that in order for him to get you to the place of expansion in your faith he had to give you a clean slate, by taking you through a journey to make you stronger.

You are who you are today because God needed to use you to see him, really see him and accept it and help you to realize it was necessary! God says I will show you how to rebuild your faith, refill your mind with my promises, Replace my trust in man with total trust in him. Repair my insecurities by teaching you how to love you with your peculiar self. I will show you how to satisfy your hunger of love by giving to you Agape Love. I will arm you with every tool to be complete in me. I will teach you how to love you, the you I created. God says I put you through Chemo because It will kill every imperfect toxic thing the enemy has implanted in you. I will allow you to go through radiation to burn all of it to make sure it does not resurface! And for every time you have a moment where you wanted to look back you will remember the crushing you had to endure. I will take away everything that ails you. I will take this time to unclog your head of years of torment. Daughter you may not see it now but you needed this I am resuscitating your life, because when I located you , you were slipping away, and I love you too much to ever let you think I wasn't there! God says I am breaking you down to nothing more than a mere cell, I am creating in you a clean and new heart so that you can see me.

See me in all of my Glory, When I placed this rare, terminal cancer on the inside of you I knew that it would make you focus solely on me! I need to show you who I am ! I need you to know that you will Defy all the odds, doctors will be stunned but you will know what I have done. I had to put you in a place where you have no choice but to seek me. You need me, because there isn't a pill that can fix this only I can. Follow my commands and you will get just what you asked me for, a more intimate praise-did you think I didn't hear you? This is for your good, don't waiver in your faith. I will surround you with Men and Women with my same heart and they will help you stay focused on me. This is spiritual communion- I will take you, break you and the bless you!

The day of surgery before prep I told my doctor I said hey listen I know that they tell you guys not to show that you're a Christian or not to act like it because it's not received by everyone but I know God told you to take me as a patient and to help bring forth his miracle, so I am telling you boldly before the throne of God that I am a Christian and I do know God so I'm going to thank you advance for allowing God to guide your hands during this procedure.

I believe only the report of the Lord, I also want to tell you what the Holy Spirit told me to tell you that the tumor that they saw on my mammogram and my ultrasound will not be the tumor that you guys pull out of me today, so don't be surprised at God's handiwork, And he smiled back at me he administered my medicine and I allowed myself to fall asleep guided by God's love. A few hours later I awoke to find someone at my bedside. I thought it was my husband because the figure that I saw when I begin to open my eyes was rubbing my hand. I felt the rubbing on my hand I finally got my eyes open and it was my doctor he standing there and he had the peace of God across his face I will never forget it. He said "hey Aisha you did great in surgery, so great in fact that every lymph node we pulled from was negative! and the most amazing part your breasts are still in tact! we only performed a partial Mastectomy it was on the side of your left breast so physically you can't see it and to the naked eye it looks normal." I highly anticipated his next word, He continued "the tumor that we pulled was only a stage one which is unheard of medically!"

(pause insert praise break, only i'm hurting so i'm dancing in my mind) and he continued "now we are waiting for the sample that we sent off to confirm the stage one but I'm almost positive that we got it all and that it is definitely a stage one and that you don't have to do chemotherapy." (GLORRRRRRRY!!!!!!) he continued "I am not a cancer doctor so I would still encourage you to follow up with her so that you can get understanding from her side what to do. If it were me I would say professionally that you don't need it, be cause of what God has just done I know you don't need it, but again listen to her and I know you will hear from God." I proceed with instruction after a few weeks of healing I go to the cancer doctor and I listen to her, but I'm also listening to the Holy Spirit, who in this moment is now speaking to me, so I can no longer hear her because his voice is loud. And he says to me "*Do the chemo because even though God has shrunk your tumor and even though the surgeon says he removed it all, the spirit of the Lord says, I am a God of excellence and I need it killed at the very root of the cell, so that you will be new you won't have to worry once you come out of this you will be a living testimony.*"

So as his voice quieted down I begin to speak while holding my husband's hand, to the doctor. "As a doctor I'm going to say to you what I said to the surgeon I trust God, I believe God, I am in total faith, I believe I am healed, I believe I am whole, and I believe that God has total control in this situation. So before you tell me I will tell you I would like to do chemotherapy followed by radiation, and now you can tell me how many cycles and then I'll schedule to meet with the radiation doctor to hear what they have planned for me. She stated that in order for me to move forward I had to have surgery yet again. This time to get a port-a-cath placed in my chest. This was so I could effectively receive the Chemotherapy. I need to go back to the surgeon and schedule this procedure.

PRINCIPLE#6 BE BOLD IN YOUR FAITH, STAND FIRM IN YOUR BELIEF OF GOD.

2 Timothy 4:2 Preach the Word (as an official messenger of Jesus) be ready when the time is right even when it is not(keep your sense of urgency) whether the opportunity presents favorable or unfavorable, whether convenient and not convenient, whether welcome or unwelcome,

(correct those who err in doctrine or behavior) warn those who sin, exhort and encourage those who are growing toward spiritual maturity with inexhaustible patience and faithful teaching.

CHAPTER SEVEN
THE CONFIDENCE

To have confidence means the feeling or belief that one can rely on someone or something; firm trust. a feeling of self-assurance arising from one's appreciation of one's own abilities or qualities.

2 Corinthians 7:16 says I rejoice that in EVERYTHING I have Perfect confidence in you.

Matthew 25:34: Then the king will say to those " Come, you blessed of my father.[you favored of God, appointed to eternal salvation], inherit the kingdom prepared for you from the foundation of the world.

LIVING AND WALKING IN YOUR PURPOSE WITH NO STRINGS ATTACHED

You now need to confident that God will do just what he says, even though your direct situation may or may not yield results and manifestations as quickly as my turn around.

So I decree and declare to you: Even If I don't have Evidence I still have Faith!

So while I was speaking with my Oncologist She said to me that I would need 6 cycles of aggressive chemotherapy. Aggressive? I don't have Cancer ma'am. I heard the Holy Spirit again *"Do the treatments God will still be by your side, he has you!"* So I agreed to the 6 cycles of Cytoxan and Taxotere set to begin starting 8/25/16, 3 days after my 9th wedding anniversary.

I continued to pray and confess without ever missing a day, or wavering in my faith. Sometimes twice a day when I felt sickness from the medicine trying to creep in. I had Big Grace hardly any side effects. I lost my hair(I was still cute though) , but I'm still Anointed! I didn't care I had my Life! I Lost All excuses during this time I was running for my life, and I was in the lead in this race. I am a winner, I always Prevail!

That's what I decided to do, Chase after God with great confidence, because he had something I wanted, because he was where my Healing came from! See I already knew what this was, God told me so. I made a vow that once I made it through my chemotherapy treatments I would be a Contagious Christian. Anyone that came in contact with me would feel the Love and Power of God through me.

I did all six treatments and aside from hair loss, that is now growing back in baby fine, I had very minimal side effects and I give all Glory to God for keeping his promise. I had gained weight during chemotherapy - the good kind. The Weight of being heavy with God's word. I am still amazed that I did not endure half of the symptoms and side effects during this time. I had to be strong. My kids really prove to step up in the area of their faith. God was healing my family. My family took good care of me. I am more than a conqueror!

Now that my chemotherapy was finished , I would now begin my daily Journey with Radiation. I had to wait three weeks to assure all of the chemotherapy was out of my system. Then I was to begin, I had to show up everyday take 10-15 min treatments and then go back home to rest, everyday except Saturday and Sunday. I completed a little over 6 weeks and at the end I rang the bell of completion. It was surreal I did have some burn but nothing like other patients that were getting treated at the same time. Most patients have severe burning and scarring once it's all said and done. I don't even have to tell you that you can't even tell where I received my radiation (Look at God Showing off)

This proved to be the best journey I had ever endured. All thanks to my God given Asthma attack in Jamaica. Don't take for granted when God tries to get your attention to slow you down. I'm grateful for everything that happened because it was all necessary to propel me forward in my chase with God. I am a Survivor I now have the Boldness to Minister to anyone who needs it. I now Love me! Every part of me. Every imperfect thing I Love me! Chasing God was by far the most exhilarating experience and know this I will always chase God! I will be a track star for Jesus! My perspective on Life will never be the same. I get a second chance at Life all because God Loved me enough to save me! Literally!

I had this awesome testimony and I exuded awesome strength but it would be remiss without scripture to back it all up. The scriptures I read on healing were the following I will list them below. What we must understand here is God is no respecter of persons what he does for one, he will do for another. If you are a believer. I believe you are! Once you get that down in your spirit you can receive anything from the father with great joy.

Isaiah 41:10- so do not fear for I am with you, do not be dismayed for I am your God. I will strengthen you and I will help you, I will uphold you with my righteous right hand.

James 5:14- Is anyone among you sick let them call the elders of the church to pray over them and anoint them with oil in the name of the Lord.

Matthew 11:28- Come unto me all of you who are weary and Burdened, and I will give you rest.

Philippians 4:19- And my God will meet all of your needs according to his riches and his Glory.

Luke 6:17-19 -Then Jesus came down with them and stood on a level place; and there was a large crowd of his disciples, and a vast multitude of people from all over Judea and Jerusalem and the coastal region of Tyre and Sidon, who had come to listen to him and to be healed of their diseases. Even those who were troubled with unclean spirits(demons) were being healed. All the people were trying to touch him, because (HEALING) power was coming from him and healing them all.

Proverbs 4:20-22- My son pay attention to what I say, turn your ear to my words; Do not let them out of your sight and keep them within your heart, for they are life to one's who find them and health to one's whole body.

Exodus 15:26-He said "If you listen carefully to the Lord your God and do what is right in his eyes, If you pay attention to his commands and keep all of his decrees, I will not bring on you any of the diseases I brought on the egyptians, for I am the Lord who heals you.

Psalm 147:3 he heals the brokenhearted and binds up their wounds (healing their pain and comforting their sorrow)

Proverbs 13:17 A wicked messenger falls into hardship, but a faithful ambassador bring healing.(watch who you have around you)

Proverbs 12:8 There is one who speaks rashly like the thrusts of a sword, but the tongue of the wise brings healing. (watch how you speak)

Proverbs 16:24 Pleasant words are sweet like a honeycomb, sweet and delightful to the soul and healing to the body.

Proverbs 17:22 A happy heart is good medicine and a joyful mind causes healing, but a broken spirit dries up the bones.(Be filled with Joy)

Mark 6:13 and they were casting out many demons and were anointing with oil many who were sick and healing them. (Be anointed with miracle healing oil)

Jeremiah 33:6 behold I will bring it to health and healing and I will heal them , and I will reveal to them an abundance of peace, prosperity, security, stability, and truth.

Psalm 107:19-20- Then they cried to the Lord in their trouble, and he saved them from their distress, He sent out his word and healed them, He rescued them from the grave. (Jesus Saves!)

Exodus 23:25- Worship the Lord your God, and his blessing will be on your food and water, I will take away sickness from among you. (He is the Truth)

Psalm 30:2- Lord my God, I called to you for help and you healed me. (Appreciation that he kept his word)

Luke 9:11 but when the crowds learned of it, they followed
him,and he welcomed them and he began talking to them
about the kingdom of God and healing those who needed to
be healed. (Teaching his people)

Isaiah 53:4-5- surely he took up our pain and bore our
suffering, yet we considered him punished by God, stricken
by him and afflicted, But he was pierced for our
transgressions, he was crushed for our iniquities, the
punishment that brought us peace was upon him, and by his
wounds(stripes) we are all healed. (Jesus Paid it ALL)

Isaiah 58:8 your light will break out like the dawn, and your
healing, restoration and new life will spring forth, your
righteousness will go before you leading you to peace and
prosperity, the glory of the Lord will be your rear guard! (He
will keep you)

Psalms 103:2-4- Praise the Lord my soul, and forget not all
his benefits, who forgives all your sins and heals all your
diseases, who redeems your life from the pit and crowns you
with Love and compassion. (Exalt him, Love on him)

Mark 5:34- He said to her, Daughter your faith has healed you, go in peace and be freed from your suffering.(because she believed his word her faith healed her) God responds to Faith!

There are so many scriptures the bible has on healing I literally could go on and on but my favorite is **3 John 1:2** Beloved I pray above all things that you would prosper and be in good physical health, just as I know your soul prospers spiritually. Heal me o' lord and I shall be healed Save me o' Lord and I shall be saved for you are my praise! **Jeremiah 17:14.**

My Love for God's word is neverending. I am at peace now in my life because of it. I do not have struggles anymore with anything that has happened to me in my life because I have been freed of those guilty transgressions. I am free of all the trauma that happened in my life. I have forgiven anyone who has ever harmed me directly or attempted to harm me indirectly. Each one of these scriptures holds a significant place in my heart, because they got me through during the time of adversity. I have so much Faith In God. His Love is never failing. No matter the circumstance my Life is in his hands, because I've got confidence in him. ~Tasha Cobbs

I have tremendous Faith that anything I ask to the Father in Jesus Name that I can have it.

My Faith is so Bold now I speak into others and because they have faith that what I'm saying is true to the word of God their Healing is Evident. I can't thank God enough for his grace and his mercy on my life. I am not worthy of all that he has done for me. My Life is full, encouraging and exciting now.

Deuteronomy 31:6 Be strong and courageous, do not be afraid or tremble at them, for the LORD your God is the one who goes with you He will not fail you or forsake you."

The Scripture will boost your confidence if you are dealing with abandonment challenges. It gives you the reassurance that God will be there so you are not alone. If you simply wanna give up, I encourage you to get this Scripture down on the inside of you for it will resonate in your spirit and bring you comfort in challenging times. If you are becoming a Christian this Scripture will give you the security that God will go before you he will protect you and he will never leave you or forsake you when you need him.

God is the mender of broken hearts so if your heart is broken give him all the pieces and just simply ask God in the name of Jesus to mend your heart and repair your emotions so that you will remember whose child you are. The Lord will be your confidence and will keep you from being caught up in this world. He will keep you safe and he will secure you in Life-Proverbs 3:26

God can help you in the area that you are challenged in, and he will give you victory over the enemy he will bring about a peace and accept you just as you are. A right relationship with God will give you the confidence to walk in your calling. We know the God causes all things to work together for the good of those who Love him and are called according to his purpose- Romans 8:28

It is very important in order to boost your confidence that you know your strengths and weakness. Find out what you enjoy doing and go with that. The bible says you can do all things through Christ that gives you strength. Pray and ask God to reveal what your purpose is and to make it plain. We are God's hands and feet in the earth. He has appointed us Evangelists and ministers unto his people, and to the unbeliever.

We ought to show love in such a way that it makes people want to serve God too. Our attitude should be positive always, because even in times of trial you can find something to learn from it. Even if it's never to repeat the same behavior or to not allow someone to treat you a certain way. We are to have a standard about us. God made us so that we have a confidence about us that no one can shake. Be strong in your spirit, build yourself up in the word and God will do the rest. 1 John 5:14 says This is the confidence that we have in approaching God, that if we ask anything according to his will that he hears us. This means whatever we ask God according to his will he will hear our request and petition. One thing though he will grant us according to his timing. So even though it may seem like you have prayed and your prayers are not being answered, have confidence that God will come through. It could be a situation where God does not think you need whatever you praying for because you aren't spiritually mature enough to handle it, or that it's simply too soon. Either way a delay is not a denial. So keep pressing forward. Do not keep praying to God about the same things over and over, we all do it.

The reason being is because when you repetitively pray it sends God a message that there is doubt in your mind that he will fulfill the request. When you pray and have doubt in the back of your mind it negates the prayer. So we should pray with confidence that the minute we pray to God in Jesus' name that we have what we receive right then. And are to act as if we already have received in preparation for that thing. Blessed is the one who trusts the Lord, and his confidence is in him Jeremiah 17:7. Do you Trust God? Hasn't he proved himself worthy of your trust? Then why would you pray with doubt? All of our sins were expunged on the cross, so there is now therefore no condemnation for those in Christ Jesus by his blood we have been set free and redeemed, God has already forgiven us for everything, you don't have to live with shame, guilt and disappointment anymore. Stop beating yourself up for things that happened in the past that you can not change. Forgive yourself. If you keep looking back you will never move ahead. There is so much more of Life to live, Let God show you how. Always remember to sow your way out. My Bishop says if you have money and it doesn't meet a need then by God almighty it must be a seed! Seed sowing is worship, and important in your walk.

PRINCIPLE#7 HAVE CONFIDENCE IN GOD

(GODFIDENCE) The assurance that no matter what is happening you are confident that God will take care of you and it. Ephesians 3:12 In him through Faith in him we may approach God with freedom and Confidence.

CHAPTER EIGHT
THE BREAKTHROUGH

Breakthrough is described as sudden dramatic and important discovery or development.; an instance of achieving success in a particular sphere or activity. To achieve your breakthrough you must maximize success. In order to maximize success you must speak it into existence. By speaking it into existence it becomes tangible. God wants us to live our best life. He tells us exactly how to do that in the bible. I have walked this Journey, I started as a broken little girl trapped in a woman's body. I couldn't even formulate a prayer when I got started, my perspective was all wrong. I lied to myself for years saying how I was delivered and the minute I opened up about my past the tears would flow. That's one way you can tell if you are truly over something is that when you speak about it you don't get emotionally enraged. I had a lot of people that I had to forgive. I always remember that forgiveness is not for the other person its for you/me. I often had to remind myself In life we have choices for everything. You will know when you are ready for a change.

You just simply choose to be happy, healthy, and whole. A broken person can not function properly. A broken person is double-minded. The bible says a double-minded person can not be trusted. I used to be so wishy-washy, undecided about everything and always sad, filled with jealousy and anger. Angry at myself because I was stuck in a rut. Jealous of others who were bold enough to invite God in and actually do and be what they wanted. I didn't have the courage to fight for myself. I would allow people to walk all over me. I didn't speak up for myself. I ruined just about every relationship I had because of fear of trust. My life was In shambles I started tithing regularly and showing God that he could trust me with my whole life including my finances. God began to show me in other areas how to change my circumstances. How to really live according to the word. I thank God that he took me in his arms and just held me. I had not been held in a long time. He broke me down so I could learn to depend on him. I have learned to be obedient to God. God says if you obey me fully and keep my covenant, then out of all the nations you will be my treasured possession, even though the whole earth is mine.

I took that literally, I was his treasured possession to me that
meant I had value on my life, and if Christ would not let
anything happen to me, then I had better learn to honor and
cherish myself as well. I meant something to God- that was
huge! Christ valued and he knew my worth. I mattered to
him so much so that he located me and saw my need and
fulfilled my life. He brought life to a dead situation. My life
was no longer hopeless but rather filled with great hope! I
have collected some confessions along my journey and I
would to share some of them with you. I have prepared some
of the confessions that have helped me become successful in
my life. You can create your own or you can use mine and
change the name or some of the wording to have it fit your
life and situation:

Confession of Confidence:

Father in the name of Jesus, I come to you now eager to start my journey of self confidence. Father you said in your word that I should not be anxious or afraid about anything, but to come to you in any situation and make my request known with prayer and thanksgiving and that your peace will over take me. God I thank you now that I have the confidence in every area of my life. I thank you that there is no condemnation toward me that I have been redeemed by you. There is no sin that I confess unto you that will go unforgiven, so father I thank you now that you have given me dominion over all things and it is rightfully mine as a believer. I thank you that I am walking in self confidence now , and that I have it by faith now because of you in Jesus' name Amen.

It is highly important walk in confidence. This confession will have you thinking you can leap tall buildings in a single bound.

Confession for Healing:

Father in the name of Jesus, I thank you for dying on the cross because it was there that healing began. I thank you Lord for being Jehovah Rophe, Lord God my Healer. I thank you for your word that covers me from my head to my feet. I thank you for making me immune to all sickness and disease for you bore it all on the cross. In the name of Jesus I rebuke any negative word that was spoken out of my mouth , or spoken to me about my health. I am healed and whole in your name. God I decree and declare that every organ, tissue , muscle , ligament , joint, vein and cell be commanded to perform a perfect work because that is what you created them to do , Father and any cell that does not line up render it ineffective and kill it now in Jesus name. Any bacteria, toxin, or other illness that tries to invade my body must go back to the pit of hell from whence it came. Lord God my body is your temple and I command it to line up as the heir to your bloodline. Satan has no place or authority over my body, Lord I am yours. I thank you that every sign and symptom of illness will not form around me, lord I cancel it now! God I thank you that you are surrounding me with your people, every physician, every technician,

Every nurse are all employed by you Jesus, everyone that you have strategically put in place obeys your will and does exactly what you tell them to do and that they have my best interest at heart, I cancel now at the root every plan the enemy tries to concoct to make me think I should live below my authority in you God. Father I thank you that your words says because I dwell in your secret place nothing by any means harm me. God I think you my health is perfect nothing missing, nothing lacking and nothing broken. Lord I thank you that I am prospering even as my soul prospers. I thank you that my youth is renewed like the eagles and I thank you that your word is true and that you have dispatched angels to protect and watch over me in the mighty powerful name of Jesus Amen.

You already know how I feel about this healing confession Jesus healed me of Cancer 30 days from the day I was diagnosed! God is faithful and his word is true.

Confession for Peace:

Father in the name of Jesus, I thank you that your peace passes all understanding. No matter what my reality is , you sit on the throne and you reign supreme you are Jehovah Shalom, the God of peace. Lord God I thank you the peace is a fruit of the spirit therefore it is my entitlement as a believer, Lord I thank you that you word declares we are to seek and pursue peace. Lord I thank you that anxiety, fear and anguish have been cancelled because you care for me and protect me. God I decree and declare that I will reap a harvest of righteousness because I am peaceful and I sow peace. Lord i thank you that my home is full of peace, My children are at peace, my husband is at peace, Lord I thank you that the evil one has no footing because I promote peace and I am full of joy. I thank you father blessing me with strength and peace. I walk in peace, I speak in peace, I believe that peace is a resident in my life now in Jesus name Amen!

Without peace you won't make it. Once you submit your will to God's He will make everything right in your life. God is a sure thing. Things that use to matter won't!

Confession for Marriage:

Father in the name of Jesus, I will take you at your and speak it out of my mouth and say that I have faith for my marriage. I believe that my marriage is blessed and favored by God. I thank God for my spouse, He/She is a gift from God and are led by the Holy spirit. I thank God that we pray together as a cohesive unit and we get manifestation. Our home is filled with Love, Peace, Honor, Humility, Respect, and Harmony. He/She loves me with the unconditional agape love that is only taught by you Lord. I thank you that we are in sync with each other and with the word of God. We are a force that can not be stopped because we believe in the power of God. We know that God honors marriage therefore we honor the union of marriage. When we disagree we quickly forgive one another and do not go to bed angry. We value each other's feelings and we talk to each other in Love. We trust each other and do not allow anyone else to have a foothold in our union.

Because God joined us together no one will separate us. I decree and declare that our marriage is stronger than ever and it is so In the name of Jesus AMEN!

So now that you have the scriptures, the confessions, and all of my principles you are well on your way to defeating the enemy. Walk in your anointing. Value your worth. You are Worth it. You are beautiful, Handsome, Smart, Intelligent, Fearless, courageous, unstoppable, and full of Faith. Can't no Devil in hell hold you back! Remember whose you are, and who you are, and that you have the power to do anything! You can change your situation around just by speaking the right things into existence. Find the version of the bible that best fits you and lets go! Me personally I was able to relate to the Amplified bible and the New Living Translation they both really made the word of God Live for me. There were times where I did need the traditional King James Version but now they even have a New King James, nevertheless find one that will keep you interested in learning more about God. Find one that will feed you the best food. Because You rock! You got this in the bag!

Grab your journal and write down all of your goals, accompanied by scriptures that coincide to what you want. Pray about each individual one. Then as you accomplish them check them off and thank God for his faithfulness. God is not a liar and he will do just what he says. He will show you his grace and mercy, Worship him! Praise him and most importantly have fun getting to know God. Have fun getting to know the new you! There will be some ups and downs but stay true to your faith and Trust God, let him lead the way. The next time a challenge presents itself you won't even flinch, because you will know what to do and you will be so connected to God you may even see it coming. Know this, the devourer is crafty and very good at his job, don't allow him to punk you out of what's rightfully yours. Don't take the bait. Don't fall for his talent of magnifying deceit! Rebuke him, Cast him down and Denounce his presence. He is a non factor in your life. Use your mouth and your heavenly language to shut him down. Remember your words shape your future. What will you build with your mouth today? Lift yourself, encourage yourself! God will rebuild, replenish and recreate you if you let him. To be transformed in Christ is to be reborn of God.

Allow him to refresh your mind and give you new perspective. The power of God will move in your life, you have to believe in him and believe in you!

Let me give you one last testimony for the road. I told you guys that I was healed of Breast Cancer less than 30 days from the date of my terminal diagnosis right? Well in addition to being healed , I didn't have to get a double mastectomy(I got to keep my boobies) because God shrunk my tumor from a stage 3 to a stage 1. On top of that my radiation so-called scars are no-more. You can't even tell I had it! God showed all the way off!

I went to a meeting at the beginning of the year, Min. Kimberly Smith, an awesome Motivational speaker, author, and Fabulous event planner had yet another successful event. This one was different though. My first big event since chemo and radiation was completed. This event, I felt compelled to go to because I was overdue to walk out my purpose. I was cute from head to toe and I was wearing a wig at the time. The question was posed to me, how would someone know that you have been through the miracle of being healed of Breast Cancer? I replied i'm not sure what you're asking, I would just tell them.

The statement was made- "looking at you , you look normal." How would we know? As I looked myself up and down I then quickly remembered and shouted "Oh my Hair!" Why are you wearing a wig then because we can't see your hair? I replied "I was trying to blend in." The minister smiled and said hmmm now that's interesting. So immediately I realized what she was talking about. I got it! Sometimes out of an attempt to " Blend In" we cover up God's handiwork, the miracle, the blessing. I unknowingly put a wig on because I wanted to be cute, but I was cute I was a natural beauty underneath. So again the question was posed to me "how would I know that you have been through Breast Cancer?" I replied "my hair? My hair, I started to cry because I got it! It sunk in. I was completely bald underneath my wig, and not because it was my haircut of choice but because of the fight and Victory I had just experienced. She asked me to remove my wig, I was reluctant but then I remembered what God had done and that had I kept it a secret no one would have known. Immediately the reaction in the room was Amazing! Life changing and it moved me to my core. Let's be honest nowadays everybody wears weave or wigs, or braids.

So the moral of this story is that in Life you must not be ashamed of who you are and what you have been through, especially when God has shown himself mighty on your behalf, we must proudly walk in such a dignified manner that others will want to know where you got this supernatural confidence. I haven't worn a wig since that day. The response I have gotten from total strangers and the ability to minister about God's goodness has been phenomenal! Don't Cover up, Let your light shine in whatever shape form or fashion it's in! Be Bold for Jesus! You too, are about to be transformed, but there is just one catch: you have to pass on your knowledge, share the Love of God and help someone else. Afterall, God didn't heal you for you to keep it to yourself! Go tell everyone you know about what God has done in your life. I am simply passing on the tools I used to get my life together. Life is what you make it. I pray that you speak into your life, and the lives of others. Be confident in who you are in God and that you will prosper and be in good health.

So in lieu of my initial process and the many changes I endured. I purposely chose the photo on the outside of the book.

To show you how I covered up, no one knew that In that time in my life I was so Broken, and unhappy. But I smiled. I wanted my readers to see what I looked like prior to my change, I wanted to leave you with a picture of what I look like now, Happy, and Beautiful. With my confident and Bold self. Pleased in my melanin skin. I am strong, Loving, Positively whole in God and a Mighty Survivor!

I am a Survivor! I am **BranNu**

AISHA D. CREWS

Brannubyaishaj-by

E.S.T.E.E.M-Owner

www.brannubyaishaj.com

For booking please call

302-359-7959

crewsaisha@gmail.com

brannubyaishaj@yahoo.com

www.ingramcontent.com/pod-product-compliance
Lightning Source LLC
LaVergne TN
LVHW051249080426
835513LV00016B/1814